ILLEGALS in America, The Epidemic

Lorraine AK Apana

PRESS

"I want to say Thank you to my husband Mel, my Son, David and to my Lord and Savior, Jesus Christ for watching over me every day in these situations". I hope and pray that I did have an impact on some of these lives, not for me, but for your glory," my heavenly Father".

He is my steadfast love and my fortress,

My stronghold and my deliverer, my shield and he in whom I take refuge, who subdues people under me.

Psalms. 144:2

Here are my stories ....

ILLEGALS in America, The epidemic

W hen I was first hired with US Immigration in the 1990's, I had no idea that the United States had so many illegal immigrants. This was an eye-opener for me, as well as I am sure it would be for many Americans. I wanted to share my experiences as a Federal Agent for US Immigration and to open the eyes of others in America at just how large the problem is in our country. I now understand why everyone that is hired as an agent or officer of US Immigration/US ICE is sent to the Immigration academy and we must learn Spanish. At the time I thought that it was a little ridiculous. My work took me on many escapades throughout the years. I had worked all over. My assignments took me too many places. Philippines, Guam, Sri Lanka, Singapore, Hungary, Germany, Tonga, Western Samoa and many states in the United States, especially the many Border towns. When I was in Baltimore, and I first became an agent, I wondered why we needed to learn Spanish because most of the illegal's that we were putting on the plane for deportation to their country were the Jamaicans. We did start to encounter illegal immigrants from Hispanic countries were in Baltimore. I was very surprised at this. Most of the people that we would encounter in Baltimore were Jamaicans. I think a lot of the

Jamaicans, believed in some type of "Voodoo" religion. I say this because of what I found in a women's purse. Since the policy was to always search the person being taken into custody, for your safety as well as theirs. During one search I was surprised when I found a dead chicken foot in the purse of a lady from Jamaica. She was very upset that we had to secure her purse out of her possession. She said she would put a "hex" on us for doing that. I said that was ok, because the God that I serve is bigger than that, and he loves her very much. She seemed perplexed, but I just always prayed that the Lord does a mighty miracle in their lives. The ironic thing is that many illegal immigrants from Mexico or a Hispanic Country had even migrated to the east coast. I even encountered when I was in Baltimore, Maryland many immigrants that were immigrating to anywhere they felt was a good place to earn money. Many did not speak English, but were happy to be making $11.00 per hour in 1995. This was a good wage for someone who was in the United States illegally. The reason why this company paid the Illegal Immigrants such a good wage was that they were to remove asbestos from the Federal Building in Baltimore.

In 1996, we were going on a raid in Maryland, Montgomery County. I was told it would be a large amount of Hispanic people that were working illegally in Maryland. We went to the Baltimore Office to be briefed on how we were going to proceed. We encountered over thirty seven Restaurants, with illegals from Mexico and two from Guatemala. We had received Intel (intelligence) that people were working from Mexico, and all of the ones employed were without the required documents to be in the country. The day long operation, extended from downtown Bethesda to Gaithersburg, Maryland. Many of the businesses were ignoring their responsibilities and would employ them anyway. Many businesses are just greedy where they could hire an illegal for under the minimum wage and save money. It was also heartbreaking that many Mom and Pop businesses would be struggling as well, and they did things the correct way by not hiring illegal immigrants. They would not hire illegal aliens even though it could be cheaper for them. The US Immigration arrested an eighteen year old girl that had been working at McDonalds for a few years. She came with her family from El Salvador five years earlier. She told US Immigration that she was not carrying her documents. This is illegal as they know that they should always carry their documents. That is their legal paperwork to be in the United States. She said that she was told that the agents could call and verify that she was in the United States legally. Clariza Esquivel said that the agents were rude. She wanted a lot of pity and wanted people to feel sorry for her. It was her responsibility to carry her documents and she knew this. You would not drive a car without a driver's license. It is the same. This raid in Montgomery County Maryland was called the "Big Chill". It ended up with 83 people arrested for being in the United States illegally. This large scale operation was rare in the Washington, D.C. Vicinity. The local National Guard was the staging area for placing the illegal Immigrants to be processed. They were photographed, fingerprinted, and given their charges to be removed from the United States. This was their legal documents stating their charges and mostly all were illegal immigrants. It was in both English and Spanish so there was no question that they would not understand it.

Speaking Spanish today is very needed with the changing of our culture. Since the United States is the closest to the country of Mexico, then we must realize that the United States is a viable entry way into our country. I could see the desperation on the illegal's face, as they would enter into the immigration office to be processed. Even while I was at the

Phoenix Airport, there were several agents coming across illegal immigrants. I noticed that "The Rock" Dwayne Johnson had come off a plane, so I asked him if I could get a photo with him and he was very nice and said yes. I never got the chance to tell him I was from Hawaii.

We would have a record of the person or persons that we had encountered in the United States that were here without proper documents, which means that they are here illegal. It was heart-breaking to see tiny babies in their arms. Many of the Mothers had a jacket on, indicating how "chilly" it was outside. Many of the babies did not have a jacket on or a blanket. The viable entry way is unbelievable since Mexico and the United States border each other. Mostly California, Arizona, and Texas border are the

states that align with Mexico. The babies in their mother's arms were very unaware of what was going on. I would continue to pray for them. Mexico has no social service system in place like the United States. There are no food stamps, or any kind of

assistance for the mothers or babies. I gave out so much of my money to the mothers from my own pocket as they would

depart from the bus. I would tell them in Spanish it was for their "nina, or nino", and not for anything else. I made it very clear to them that their young child needed Milk and Diapers. Most of the Mothers seemed very grateful, but I could not help but wonder what their living situation was like. It was very heartbreaking to see this. I would leave them with a prayer and ask that the Lord keep his hand on them. These boys we were feeding, but they were found wandering in the desert alone. They seemed relieved when someone found them and to have food. We Americans are so lucky and blessed, to have so much freedom. We should be thankful and realize that we have so many freedoms that others do not have. The United States was founded on Christian Values, and we should be so thankful that the Lord, our God has blessed us here with this. When I was borrowed for Tucson, Arizona, a few of us officers from other stations got together and decided to go down to "Nogales", to shop and have a great authentic Mexican meal. While we were in Nogales, we could see how hard these people worked, even in the small restaurant that we went to had women in the back as we could see making hand tossed tortillas. It was very sad to see the little children four or five years old, selling chicklets gum on the street. The little boys and girls could barely speak their broken English to say "chicklets". I would always buy one or two because I knew they had to eat also. Many people or vendors were out on the street to sell their wares, goods, or even food on the street. Mothers, with small babies, would cook right on the street with their babies in tow. Many of the stands that were set up were very rickety, but the mothers would keep them as clean as they could.

Back in the mid-1990's working on the Border I did not feel threatened or concerned at all. I knew that I had the Lord on my side, but people seemed to be more respectful in their country and the culture was different then what it is today. Today it is very different, with more crime, illicit activities and a lot more drug activity for quick money. Sadly there are very few jobs in Mexico, to make a good living. Education seems to be either beyond most of the financial needs of the countries citizens. Today you would need to worry about teaching at one of the schools in Mexico, as the drug dealers are threatening many of the teachers. The drug cartels or dealers are telling the teachers give them a portion of their monthly income if they want to live. Many are being threatened that they will be kidnapped, their family kidnapped, or they will be killed. This was not the case before, but the drug cartel or people just trying to sell drugs for money are finding an easier way to get money. I fear that many Americans have taken so many of our freedoms for granted. We are truly a blessed nation and country, and we need to remember where our rights have come from. The Lord has his hand on our Country. At least I want to believe that he still does.

Most of the people coming from Mexico are raised Catholic, but the few that I spoke to did not always go to Mass, or tried to go when they could. They had told me that they believed in God, but did not understand why things turn out the way that they do.

When I was borrowed to the various Border Patrol Offices in Arizona and California, these would be the areas we would work because they are the hardest hit regions for an assignment. This would be to assist in the south west. I would spend assignments being borrowed to Tucson Arizona. The other places that I have gone to are Phoenix Arizona, Casa Grande, El Centro, California, and Wilcox Arizona. I also have been on an assignment to Midway Island that I will talk about later.

One of my assignments while on assignment would be to find out

Which one of the shifts I would be working. When I was on the day or the morning shift, I would usually go down the street to Burger King. The Burger King had a contract with us to provide good breakfasts for the people that we had in custody. We had no way of knowing when there last meal was. It was very healthy and they seemed to love it. It would consist of Orange Juice, egg breakfast jack, and potatoes. Everyone usually asked for more, and if we had it we would provide it to them instead of throwing it away. We would also put water in a container and have it in the cell so they could drink whenever they got thirsty.

One of my other Jobs would be to load the Immigration Bus with 52 detainees to transfer back to the border. I knew that the Lord was with me and I will tell you why. It was a regular big bus, like a school bus, except it said "US Immigration" on the side. It was outfitted with a toilet in the rear, and a locking cage between the driver and the detainees. When I was borrowed, and we could see that personnel were in short supply, I would load up the bus with one of the supervisors and start off into the cold air towards Nogales Mexico. The port of Entry was the destination for all the illegal immigrants from Mexico being returned to their country. When they would get off of the warm bus because I had the heater on for the many people, then they would get off into the cold night air, I would hope and pray that their destination would be close by. Many of them I knew came from other States in Mexico, many a lot further than I was taking them to. The bathroom in the back had toilet paper, but no door. There was a makeshift curtain put up over the door for privacy. When I would drive the bus loaded to the border, I knew that God was with me because you can look at the picture and see how many there were, where they were let out and how if the Lord was not with me I could have very well been over ran by the illegal immigrants that were getting off of the bus. The Illegal Immigrants could have taken my pepper spray, sprayed me with it, this would have disabled me and then took my weapon. They could have

beat me up, and taken my gun from me to shot and kill me. I was not though, and I know that is only by the grace of God that I was not.

Most of the illegals that I was taking back were originally picked up in the desert by the Border Patrol Agents. When they were picked up, they were hand-cuffed, because we do not know what their his-tory includes. We photo-graph, fin-g e r p r i n t , feed them, and let them use the rest-r o o m . Before they are taken back to their c o u n t r y

border, we will give them a copy of the notice, explaining their rights in English and Spanish. It was explaining that if they are caught again in the United States, they could do jail time for being a "reentry Offender" without the correct documents needed to come into the United States.

When asked if they would try to come into the United States again, all that were asked said "Yes" they would. They said that if they made it to the United States without getting caught that they had nothing to lose. When I would get to the border, I knew the hand of God was on me because you can see from the pictures; they had all of their belongings under the bus in the holding compartment. Unless I dropped them at a point of entry where there were Immigration agents there, I would be alone, and a lot of times it was ten or eleven o'clock at night. It was very dark, I was alone to them, but me myself I knew that my Lord my Savior was right there with me at those times. Many times I would travel from Tucson to the Border with a full bus load. I would go three or four times in a shift. This was only one little station. It makes you think how many illegal's each station must have, or encounter and now the new threat of armed drug dealers they must contend with.

Many were told with the paperwork that they were given if arrested they would face jail time. Jail time however, in the United States is a cake walk for the immigrant. They would receive three meals a day, have recreation and exercise time. Hot showers, school classes, and religion are just a few of what is offered to them. Although many do not follow the Christian religion, many turn to some other religion. I would hope and pray that they would find peace with following the Lord and getting a Bible to read while they are incarcerated. Supervisors were very knowledgeable, helpful, and understood the job we were doing. I think that this helped knowing the Supervisor knew what we were up against. While I was in Arizona there was a supervisor that was arrested. This was not the first time that I heard this while I was there. This supervisor had worked for Border Patrol for 23 years. He was arrested for selling maps on where the sensors were placed in the desert to the drug dealers and smugglers of human cargo. The sensors were buried out in the desert in known remote areas where they knew that illegal immigrants were known to travel. These little sensors are very expensive and are hooked up in the Border Patrol main office. These sensors are very high tech and would only alert the agents in the Border Patrol office if it was a group of people walking in a remote area. It would not alert if it was an animal or something smaller than a person. I do not know how much money the supervisor was paid for this information, but I cannot believe that he compromised the Border Agents safety and put many people in danger as the illegal immigrants knew where the sensors were located. A lot of people give in to the temptations that the evil one lays out for us. The sensors alert the Station that a sensor has gone off. You can detect whether a large group is travelling or a small group is travelling. Most groups travel with what little possessions that they have. Many also make sure that they have water in plastic jugs, and when they drink all of the water, they discard the plastic jugs. In the desert it is now filthy and litter is strewn all over. In the Arizona paper in 2002, there were four articles about different Border Patrol Agents that were arrested. They were arrested on serious charges and activities. Agent Hemmer was arrested of kidnapping and sexually assaulting an alien before removing her back to Mexico. One Border Patrol Agent was charged with assault and arrested, but the case was dismissed after a year. Agent Johnson had held a Supervisor position, but was charged with felony count of kidnapping and sexual assault on a 23 year old El Salvadoran woman who was in custody. In Arizona, there are a lot of Native American reservations. Many Native American Indians would report to the Border Patrol when a group of illegals were traveling across their land. The American Indians were helpful in this respect so they would know where the group was traveling and approximately the size. The American Indians did not like the groups that trekked across their reservation to just discard their empty jugs and leave them there. That is why there is so much trash and rubbish just left out in the desert. Since we are often borrowed for a different station that is short of the much needed personnel, Officer's can be farmed out to Border Patrol Stations or to a major prison as well in Arizona. Florence Prison in Arizona has a high immigration population with illegals in the prison. It could be because of a crime that the person committed, waiting for their court date with the immigration judge.

****

In El Centro, California, I worked with Border Patrol Agents at the checkpoints, and also along the railroad tracks. When an approaching train was arriving, the conductor would slow the train down so that we could shine our flashlights. We would usually run along side of the train so if we saw bodies, we could give them commands to get off the train. Some would jump, but a few would jump and then take off running into the desert. I was surprised there was always illegal's hiding on the train. The illegal's that hid on the train were trying another venue into the United States. We would always do a pat down on someone we arrested. We would look for drugs, contraband, and weapons. I was patting down a group of detainees for drugs or weapons. I found a lipstick on a detainee that we had in our group. I asked him why he had a lipstick. One of the other agents told me to take the top off. When I did I was surprised to see a very sharp knife

that had been glued into the bottom of the lipstick. This was a very sharp knife; it could have injured or killed someone.

I was surprised we had even caught three illegal men travelling with a group of illegals through the desert. What was surprising was these men were from Poland. It is easier to get into Mexico and use it for a stepping stone into the United 'States. This picture depicts just how easy it is to come into the United States with a

load of Marijuana. The man that was driving this vehicle in the desert, when the Border Patrol tried to pull him over, he jumped from the vehicle and began to run in the desert. They were unable to catch him and the reason why the vehicle was loaded with so much Marijuana. This happens quite a lot.

****

I was also borrowed for the Florence Prison in Arizona. There were a lot of illegals transferred to this prison. This whole road was nothing but prisons, up one side and another. Some of the prisons were classified as maximum, and others were mimimum. Most of the immigration inmates were kept in Florence. This was more of a logistic maneuver. Immigration at that time wanted to keep them in one location. This worked pretty well, but not for all of the inmates. I was working at the Florence facility and I also had the duty of watching the inmates during their lunch time. All of us officers had to stand at the wall to watch the detainees eat and to not cause any problems. I was standing in the back next to the wall, when one of the inmates was cleaning off the tables. This one detainee smiled and said "Hi". I also smiled and said Hello to him. The Lord touched me and I decided to tell him that "There was nothing that he had done that the Lord Jesus Christ could not forgive him for". At this moment I was startled at what he did. He said to me: You said the "J" word, so I have to leave. It does say that in the Bible, that when you say the name of Jesus, the devil has to flee. This showed me how much power is in the name of Jesus as it says in the Bible. This proved it to me. I pray for the officers, but also for these inmates. If they knew Jesus, then they would know they are forgiven and lead others to Jesus.

****

When I was detailed to El Centro, California, I was working in their El Centro Border Patrol Office. It was next to the El Centro Prison. There were so many illegal's that I did not know I would have so much overtime, and also be so tired from working so much. El Centro is only 11 miles from Mexicali Mexico. The largest city in Imperial County is El Centro. In 2010 there was a 2010 census conducted and at that time the population was 42,598. It is a flourishing agricultural area. El Centro is one of the most productive farming regions in California. The annual crop in California produces over one billion in fresh produce. We were always working and I am not even sure how much of a dent we were making. It seemed like at every road or in the desert there were illegal immigrants trying to make their way into the United States. El Centro is a small farm town not far from Mexico and close to the border at Yuma Arizona. At Yuma there is a marine base and it is extremely hot in the summer time. Since I had so many opportunities while working at El Centro, I had invited my Son and his friend from high school to come on an observation. My Son thought at one time he would like to work as a Border Patrol agent. Both of the boys came down to El Centro, and the Supervisor was going to take them out to a farm area at night to show them what the work consisted of. This was approximately 2300 at night. It was very dark, it was pitch Black. No Street lights, no lights whatsoever. My Son and his friend went with the supervisor and could not believe what they were seeing. In the huge farmland with vegetables growing and spread out, when the cars head lights and flood lights shone on the farm area, you could see all the illegal's scattering and hiding in what little spaces there were under the vegetables and trying not to be seen. There were so many illegal's when the lights were shone under all of these spaces, there were so many and they would jump up to run and be scattered. In the summer time, June, July, and August are the hottest months in El Centro,

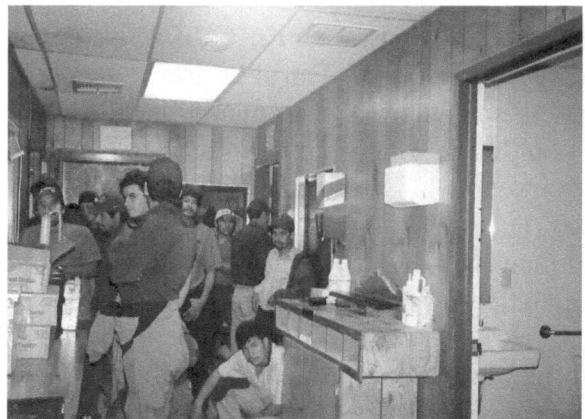

California. During these months the temperature hovers at 121 or 122 degrees. During these months, many of the illegal's the border to California had to be taken to the hospitals for dehydration, sun stroke, or just feeling week. I would tell them in Spanish that I would pray for them. Many were grateful to still be alive and they were not very old. Many were in their twenties, or thirties. When it is so hot, and they run out of water it is a desperate situation.

While I was working at El Centro Border Patrol Station, I had the opportunity on my day off to go up with the Border Patrol Agent who was the helicopter Pilot. I would be the "spotter". What this basically meant was that we were looking for groups of illegal's trying to make their way through the desert. When we would see a group of immigrants trying to transverse in the desert, we would try to see if it was accessible by vehicle. If it 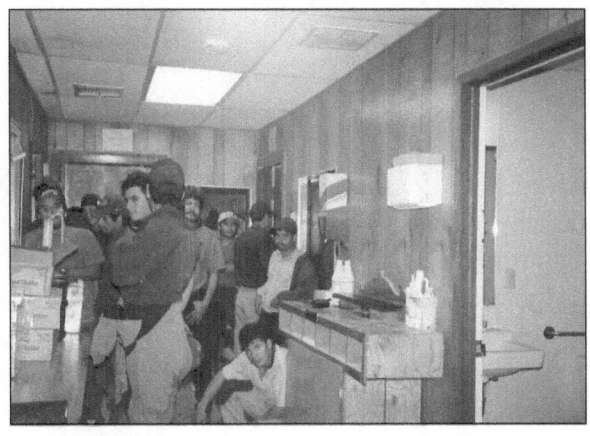 looked accessible, we would radio for assistance. While we were up in the air, we did have a vantage point where we could see the people easier. Many times when we would see a group and they realized that we were the Border Patrol, the group would scatter, trying to hide under trees, boulders, or any place they could. Being high in the air you can see the different colors of clothes. Although they thought that they were hiding, they actually were not because of their colors of clothes.

A couple of times we were in an area that was flat enough to radio for the Immigration Bus to come to the area. The reason why this would happen would be that there were too many illegal's for a Border Patrol Vehicle to carry. At times the most dangerous part picking that many up was that there was so many people, and the most Immigration Agents that were there was about five or six with about thirty or forty illegals. If we could access the area with the Immigration Bus then I

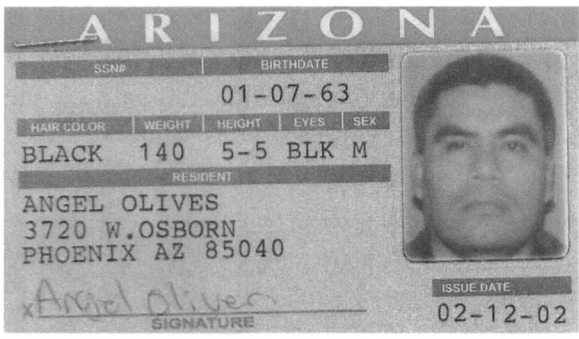

would drive out to where the agent was with many of the Illegal Immigrants. Once we were able to put them on the bus we could take them back to the Border Patrol Station for processing. It was good to get back to the station with the illegal immigrants because they had all been traveling for so long, desperately needed a shower, clean clothes and sleep. You could smell the stench in the air, and the heater on the bus to keep them warm made the smell worse. In many remote desert areas as these, the agents would ride the ATV's or quad runners. This was transportation that was accessible to these areas. Many times in the El Centro area the agents would receive word that an illegal van or vehicle with either illegals that they could see a shadow of, or if the truck was low in the back with a tarp over the back, it could be a suspicious vehicle. Sometimes in the dark, when it was confirmed that it was an illegal vehicle with suspicious cargo, when they tried to stop the vehicle they would not stop. In cases like this, if the Border Patrol Agent knew the direction that they were heading, they

would try to set up with a spike strip across the highway. If it was dark enough most vehicles could not see the spike strip across the road and would run over it. When this occurred their tires would be fattened by the spike strips. Many  would jump out of the vehicle and start to run. When they "heard the word, Policia" in Spanish over the vehicles public

address (PA) system, they would stop. The Border Patrol agents would take them into custody and the driver of the vehicle  would be charged with additional charges. Most of the drivers of the vehicle would be sentenced as being the smuggler. Many are called the "Coyote Smuggler". Many of the people that were encountered were from Mexico, Guatemala, Brazil, and other Latin American countries. This did not stop them from travelling so far to try to come to the United States. The sad thing is that many of the illegals from Mexico or other Hispanic countries had to pay to obtain a false identification. Most of

these Identifications were used to secure a job and they either use their correct name or use a false one on the identification. In the United States, most people realize that they must have a form of ID to be able to get a job. So even if there identification is false, or a counterfeit, or they do not know how to drive they can get a drivers license easily and they know that they can at least get a job. People that are incarcerated in the United States are very blessed. Not only are they allowed going to the worship service of their choice, there is Bibles that are given out to them freely. They are entitled to three meals a day, exercise time, television time or just free or relaxed time. In the Mexican prisons, I have been told by supervisors that unless their relatives or family bring them food, their meals will consist of bread, water, or rice. This is all that is provided to them in Mexico, so they are treated very well in the United States.

****

Taking a suspected Terrorist to Sri Lanka was a very long and tiring trip. This trip was one of the most taxing trips I had been on. One of my co-workers and I had to take this suspected terrorist all the way back to his home country, which was Sri Lanka. He was a belligerent, angry, and very antagonistic person. This person was trying to attend the flight school in Florida, where the world trade center bombers had attended. The 9-11 suspects went to this location to learn to fly planes. The hijacked jets on September 11, 2001, were well thought out and sophisticated act of terrorism on United States soil. This was going to be a long flight. We flew from Hawaii to Japan to change aircraft to travel on to Sri Lanka. When we arrived at Nagoya Airport, we were told that "Nippon" airlines would not let us board. The main reasons were the flight crew noticed the man we were deporting home was carrying a flight bag. This is the same identical bag that pilots carry and also the pilots that hijacked the American and

United Airlines to carry out their devastating plan on September 11, 2001. The Nippon pilots decided they did not want to take us given all the flags that were going up in their minds. Because the Pilots refused to let us board the plane, the Japanese Police sgt, came out and was very helpful. He was very compassionate and professional as well. They took our deportee to a jail cell overnight, and I and my partner were taken to a hotel that was close to the airport. We got a good night's rest, and we were put on another flight. It was a different airline, and

we had to go to Singapore first. Our Detainee was agitated and belligerent all of the way, when the Japanese Police brought him back to us so we could finish the escort to Colombo, Sri Lanka. This illegal that we were taking home (Dissanayake) had been on the Philippine Airlines Flight, PR-103 when they had a refueling stop in Honolulu, continuing onto California. He looked more Middle Eastern than Sri Lankan or Indian. He had been very argumentative with the flight crew and assaulted a member of the flight crew. He interfered with the crew as they were trying to perform their duties. When the plane landed in Hawaii, at the Honolulu International Airport, He was arrested. He had an Immigration Hearing and was ordered removed by the United States Immigration

Judge. Taking him back was not easy, and required a lot of prayer on my behalf. When we finally arrived in Colombo, we were both so exhausted and ready for rest. My partner and I had different reservations at the Hotels in Colombo, Sri Lanka. When I got out at the Hilton, I had some money in my pant pocket, and the very nice taxi driver had already set my small backpack out of the trunk. I went into the Hilton, and at that moment I realized that I had left my purse in the taxi. It had my passport, credit cards, airline ticket and everything else. I could not pay for my room, and was extremely tired. I called my Husband collect and explained tearfully what had just happened. We immediately lifted this   situation and the taxi driver in prayer. We asked the Lord to intervene on my behalf. The Lord heard our prayer. The Gentleman had stopped at a store and noticed my bag in the back seat He came back. I told him to come back in the morning to take me to the airport. I gave him a big tip, as he was very nice. I asked him what religion he was and I was surprised to learn that he was a Buddhist. I had not   before that realized that there were so many Buddhist in Sri Lanka. I knew that Sri Lanka had many rebel groups, like the Tamil Tigers, but encountering a Buddhist was a shock to me. When I thought of Buddhist, I thought of Japan, not Sri Lanka. I was surprised to learn that 70% of all Sri Lankans are Theravada Buddhists. The remainder is such. 15% are Hindus, 7.5% are Muslims and the remainder of 7.5 % is Christians.

****

I had a trip to Budapest, Hungary with a man coming from Hawaii on numerous child molestation charges. I and my co-worker had to go with him all of the way to Budapest to escort him on the plane and to keep a watch on him that he wasn't a nuisance. This was a long trip, as we had to fly from Hawaii to New York, then the next day we would transit

Malev Airlines then onto Hungary. The US Government policy is to send two officers with the convicted person so that the US Immigration will not liable if we send them alone and they cause a problem or accost someone. I was elated to see in our church magazine that there are many people in Budapest that are on fire for the Lord. That was an awesome testimony to see. I did not witness this when I was there in the year 2000. I had prayed for the people and this country, and God answers prayers.

****

In 1998, I was in Medford, Oregon working. I was very surprised that when we went out on a raid, that it could turn very deadly. In May of 98, at about 11:00 pm, a lot of us officers were on a raid of a company called "forest Products Company. This company was known to hire illegals and had many working for their company. We all drove up in a convoy of Government vehicles, since we did not know how many we would arrest. One of the Special Agents that was with us, observed a man sitting in his vehicle with the engine running. The Special Agent was tapping on the rolled up window, and "asking him to please turn the engine off." There was not response, but the Agent continued tapping on the rolled up window. At this point everyone was waiting for the person in the vehicle to comply with the orders given and to turn the vehicle off. It was at this moment that the vehicle gunned the engine, and immediately took off forward. The agent kept yelling at the vehicle to stop. The vehicle was heading straight for all of us officers at a high rate of speed. We all had to jump out of the way of the vehicle or we would have been hit because he was at a high rate of speed. The vehicle kept moving at a very high rate of speed, I had my pen and wrote down this license number on my hand. They ran the license, and looked for the person driving this vehicle. I do not know if he was ever arrested. That was a very thankful night as God was watching over all of us. The vehicle could have come straight at us and we could have all been killed.

Many times in Medford, Oregon we would have to drive the Immigration Bus up to Portland, Oregon approximately a four hour drive. Along the way up to Portland we would at times stop in Roseburg at the Border Patrol Station. If they had suspected illegal's we would take them with us. This morning we did not have anyone to pick-up so we proceeded onto Portland.

When we arrived in Portland, Oregon we noticed that there were many men to be transferred to a secure location. This would mean a local Jail, or ready to be deported. I noticed as we were escorting the men out the back door to the secure vehicle, there was one man who had handcuffs on and ankle chains as well. He was from Nigeria, and he had only been arrested a couple of days before. He suddenly lay on his back and started trying to kick and spit. I and the other officer told him to stop resisting, and to get up off the ground. He would not. We kept trying to reason and talk to him, but he would not listen. At that moment, I stepped back, pulled my pepper spray out, and shouted "spray" as we are taught to do before we spray anyone. After I sprayed him, he became more compliant. After we were able to pick him up, we needed to clear the spray out of his eyes with fresh water. He was a lot calmer, but he called me some evil names. I will not repeat these names, but he reminded me of Pharoh in the Bible. He wanted his way. Many times in Oregon, we had raids set up on local businesses that would hire illegals. The local law Enforcement intelligence had been giving the Supervisors good information. I was actually surprised at how many illegals we really had in Oregon, let alone in the United States. That morning in May of 1998, there were forty of us agents that would make a long nine hour raid onto different businesses. There were two restaurants, in Eugene, Oregon where four people were arrested. There were 9 others arrested at the local market, called "La Fiesta Market". The restaurants were Centennial Steak House, and Playa Azul Restaurant. The Majority of illegals arrested were at Emerald Forest Products. The arrested 35 illegal immigrants that had collectively earned one Million dollars. It did not assist our economy because most of the earned money was sent back to Mexico to assist their families. This money did not stay in our economy but instead went back into the Mexican economy.

****

I and another Officer were going to take four illegals to California to be removed back to their home country of Mexico. We were travelling on United Airlines flight #54 to Los Angeles. We were leaving late at night, 2245 military time or at 10:45 P.M. The males were all compliant except one. His name was Antonio Lugo-Moron. When we boarded the aircraft, and we had already made arrangements for assigned seats at the back of the plane, myself and the other officer had to repeadly ask him to take his seat. He was standing up, very fidgety. The regular passengers had not started boarding the aircraft yet, but we were given information that they would start boarding. He kept leaving his seat, and we had to continually bring him back. He asked one of the flight crewmembers if he could have a cigarette. The flight crew continually reminded him that this was a non-smoking flight and it was against Federal Regulations to smoke on an aircraft, especially when this was a pre-flight brief. When we asked him to take his seat numerous times, he became more and more agitated, and his voice would go higher. Lugo-Moron then tried to be combative with my partner. He pushed my partner that was with me, and tried to be very combative and physical. We both held him down on the floor of the aircraft and proceeded to put handcuffs on him. We had just got him escorted back to his seat; put the seat belt on him when he started yelling. He was yelling obscenities at my partner and me. The other three Men that we were escorting were compliant and could not understand this man. Lugo-Moron began yelling loudly and obscenities. We had to ask him to cease because there were little children on the aircraft and also he was drawing attention to himself. He was swearing in English and Spanish. He said that he wanted "to kill us". I knew then that he was acting like he had a "demon" in him. The Captain of the United Flight #54 told the flight attendant to let us know that he had already radioed for Airport Police to meet us at the gate when we arrived. He also had the US Immigration at the Airport to be notified and contact the office to send assistance. When the Aircraft had pulled up to the Jet way, we were met by Local Law Enforcement officers. They were assisting to remove the suspect off of the plane. Even while the police were escorting him to a waiting vehicle, he continued to yell, and was yelling "Help", someone help me. The witnesses, like the Pilot, and other crewmembers were told that they would probably be contacted as this would go to a federal Court trial. The Federal Bureau of Investigation (FBI) was also notified. All the witnesses that were on the aircraft said they would be willing to make an official statement of the incident that took place.

****

A 23 year old man from the Island of Micronesia had come to Hawaii, because the United States has a treaty with the Federated States of Micronesia and Marshallese Islands. The United States gives money to these people because they let us use their land during the bombing of Pearl Harbor. This man from Micronesia, was named Forgive Otokichy and he, was living in Hawaii with his girlfriend and working part-time. This case was referred to Adult Probation because his Immigration status was unknown. Because he entered the United States, on the "Compact of Free Association", he would not need a Visa. He did have tattoos located on both of his arms, left and right. He had actually gone to court for a hearing on sexual assault in the second degree. He was sentenced to one year in Prison and then he would be removed back to Micronesia. He was ordered Removed and to be Deported back to Micronesia. Micronesia is a very poor country, and it seems as if these people do not strive to get an education, or go to college. I had been to Ponpei and Chuuk in their country. Both were beautiful Islands with beautiful sea waters rolling in. Ponpei was a little more tranquil than and not as busy as Chuuk. It did not seem that Ponpei needed roads fixed as bad as Chuuk. Chuuk is also more populated. Kosrae was a beautiful Island just landing there, but I never had to stay on Kosrae. I would have liked it.

Taking illegals back to the Philippines was another opportunity to really see what these people were escaping from. Many had had a relative to sponsor them to come to the United States. Most of the people that came to the United States were blessed that they had a relative to sponsor them to come to the United States. The sad thing is that many had the chance and

opportunity to get a relative to sponsor them to come into the United States. For one reason or another, mostly hanging with the wrong crowd, they had got into trouble that was considered an Immigration violation and the Immigration Judge had ordered them removed. Because most of their crimes were serious in nature, they were ordered removed with an escort. There are only two that I remember being females to removed to their native country. All of the rest I remember as being "Male".

At one time the Government had contracted a plane to fly from, California, then onto Hawaii, and the final destination would be Clark in the Philippines. This was an old Air Base; they had the room for the plane to land and the area to process the people that were removed from the United States. This air base was on the southern tip, approximately 4 hours south of Manila. These were all the Filipinos that had seen the United States Immigration Judge, and had been ordered removed back to their home country. We had approximately 105 to be removed from the United States back to their home country. There were approximately thirty officers on the plane, and the Filipinos that we were removing back to the Philippines. On the air craft, they would be hand cuffed, and they could use the planes restroom. If the hand cuffs needed to be removed then we would station two officers outside the bathroom door. The hand Cuffs could be repositioned to their clothing so they could have their hands free. It was sad to look at each one of their faces, many young, still in their twenties. The sad thing is that they fell to the temptation that the Devil had put in front of them. If many of them had the "real Jesus" in their heart, then I do not think they would have done what they did.

Once we cleared the aircraft, disembarked all the personnel we had brought, along with unloading their personal property. It would be a four hour drive for the officers and we would have to have tandem vehicles because we did not have enough space or a bus to carry everyone. The closer we were getting to the City of Manila, you could see the congestion, the cars would come so close to each other that you could literally reach out and touch the next vehicle. There are no lined roads like ours, everyone just drives were they can. This is a very poor country, however there hotels are beautiful. Most people that I had encountered were humble and sorry for their mistake. Most Filipinos that I encountered were Roman Catholics, but many are stepping out to new "Christian" Churches that are moving in the areas. They did realize that being a Christian you could have a personal relationship with the Lord Jesus Christ. I was also very surprised that in Manila the malls are huge. The older mall that I went to was four or five stories high. We do not have malls that big in the United States. I had also just heard that they built the "Mall of Asia". This mall has an ice skating rink, and from what people had said it would take two days to see this mall. I did not have the opportunity to see this mall, but there are others as well. I was also amazed that while in "Robinsons" mall, I had a Middle Eastern man following me around. I do not know why. Only the Lord knows and protected me. At one point I finally turned around and said" What do you need"? He looked startled and left. I know that the Guardian angels were protecting me. I was relieved and thanked my Lord and savior when I saw him walk to the exit.

****
****
****
****

Tahiti was a place I had always wanted to go. The pictures did not do justice for Tahiti. I was blessed and had the opportunity to go with my boss to deport a man from there. I was thankful for this opportunity to go to Tahiti. The first thing that I noticed about Tahiti was how expensive it was. I was there almost five years ago now, and the price of a Coca-cola in the can was $3.00 then. I am sure it is more now. Tahiti reminded me a lot of Hawaii. I spoke to the girl that worked in my hotel, and she said that yes, it was very expensive, and she worked three jobs just to make ends meet. Many of the people I spoke with had to work two or three jobs just to survive. Most families live with one another to help the situation. I know that the food I had for dinner was over thirty dollars for a hamburger and French fries. I was surprised that their culture is very different. I went down to the sea shore, and I did not realize that Tahiti is still maintained by the French. Most of the people on the beaches were topless. This was a shock to me, so I went back to my Hotel. I did not see any churches close to where I was, but the Phone book I looked at had a few.

****

Several different Immigration offices were notified that there was a boat adrift calling for "Mayday". The Coast Guard that had picked up the "Mayday" signal said that the man making the "Mayday" call was in broken English. The engine had stopped working and the boat was adrift. The captain of the craft said that he had tried to start the engine many times, but just could not get it to work. It was not until the next day that the Coast Guard was able to make contact with the vessel. The Coast Guard docked next to the boat. They could hear yelling and screaming coming from below on the ship. When the Coast Guard went below to surmise the situation, they were astonished at what they found. They found young girls, young boys, men and others in the cargo access area. It was cramped, dark, and filthy. They had no food or water. It

also appeared that they did not have a place to sleep and had to go to the bathroom anywhere they could.

The Coast Guard surmised that going to Midway Island was the closest and the only place that the Coast Guard plane could land with provisions. This is where I would fly into and stay on Midway Island

for two Months. I was transported by the Coast Guard from Ewa Beach in Hawaii. It was told by many of these Chinese that the Juveniles from

China were going to go to the East Coast; probably they said "to work in a restaurant". When the Smuggler's were apprehended and interviewed it came out that they were going into "Sex Slavery" in the New York Area. They would basically be indentured servants, or sold into prostitution. The good work conditions that they were told of were not the truth. They thought that they were going to work in

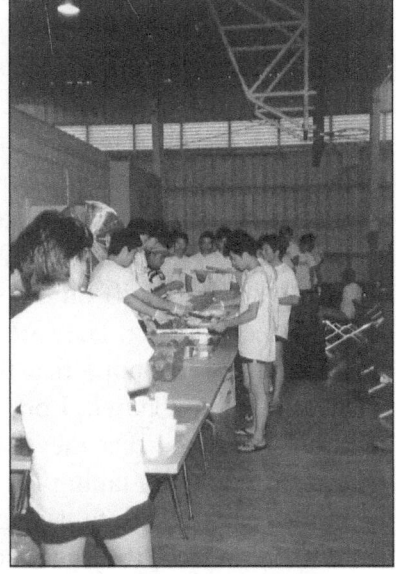

restaurants. They did not know that they were really going to be sold into "Sex Slavery" in the New York City Area.

They also liked that in "America", you could have more than one child. One of the girls who spoke pretty good English, I spoke to. She said that "Girl Babies" are not valued. They cannot work in the fields or help with working on the farm. It was sad that they would find "girl babies", many times just dumped by the side of the road. The deplorable conditions that were on the ship to travel to the United States were horrible. In pictures 18 and 20, you can see the terrible conditions that they had to travel in. In 21 they are standing against the fence to pray. They were Buddists.

I think about many times if the ships engines had not failed or died, then what kind of life would they have had. They probably would not have been encountered by the US Coast Guard. I was in charge of watching the juveniles on the tennis courts under the tents. Many of these girls and boys were very young, and they had no clue what was in store for them. Many said that they did not know where they were going or what kind of job they would have. The Chinese Government was sending a 747 aircraft to Midway Island to pick up the illegals that were adrift on the ship. They would be removed and returned to China. They are devout Buddhists, but I would pray for them, and hope that they might find a good underground Christian Church. I pray that the Lord would have his hand on them, and that they have a good life. The men that were instrumental in taking the money from them to travel to the United States were to be charged in Federal Court. I never heard how long that they had received incarceration for. Many store for them. Many of the young girls and boys were crying boarding the aircraft. They did not know what was going to happen to them, or where they were going. We never heard what did become of them or where they were sent back to. Prayer is Powerful, so that is all I can do to give me comfort is to know that I asked God to protect them.

****

In 1996 or 1997, I went to Bangkok, Thailand. We had to escort a man that was actually from Laos back home, but Thailand was as far as the Country would let us go. When we got to Bangkok, we escorted him to the gate to fly to Vientiane, in the country of Laos. We do not know what happened with him either as we were not given any information or a contact that we could call. Thailand was hot and humid. Like most countries it had its good areas and it's not so good areas also. The Hotel was across the street from the mall, and our accommodations were very nice. The corner of our Hotel, nightly you could see "temple dancers". These women were Buddhist. These were the women from their different temples that would come and light incense, dance, and say a prayer. They were very rigid in their performance but I was told that they really believed what they were praying for would come true. They also had a Palace in Thailand that is a monument in their Country. One of the Princes had lived there, and they had every kind of Buddha you could imagine. There was the "reclining Buddha", the "emerald Buddha and various other Buddha's". This palace was built in 1783, and was also the royal residence. When the Country of Siam restored law and order after the fall of Ayutthaya who was the monarch at this time, then Bangkok took over. This palace is claimed to be the World's Largest Golden Teakwood mansion. It is Beautiful, but these people do need to know God and Jesus in a Personal way.

****

In 1998, I was sent to the Island of Guam for 2 ½ months to work with the Kurdish Refugees. I had never dealt with  Muslims or even had heard of them let alone know what their beliefs were. While I was on Guam I was to assist with the ones that were being processed into the United States. The Coast guard had already alerted the US Immigration and these were the Kurdish refugees coming to seek safety. It was reported that when Saddam Hussain was alive that he wanted to kill the Kurdish Refugee's. When the couples were brought in it was a different culture for them. They had to have a place to stay, so many were relocated to base housing that was empty. They did not know that in America you cannot beat or hit your wife. The Military Police were called  to many of the residences were the Husbands were physi- cally beating or slapping their wives. The men had a hard time believing that this was not acceptable in the United States. They wondered about America, and "how we kept our wives in line". This was a shocking revelation for the Middle Eastern Men.

They believed in their Koran and that "Allah" said that it was ok to strike your spouse. Many of the Muslims came from a Southeastern city of Diyarbakir. Most were resettled to different States and Cities in America. The reason that US Immigration and the State Department brought them over is they felt it would be better and easier to bring the Kurds to Guam and "Parole" them in. Paroling them in is an Immigration Term that the United States would have an easier time to locate them into the United States. Since they would not have a Visa, it would be easier to process them on Guam. This was easier to do, because if they had been processed in the United States, they would need to have all of their documents, interviewed, processed and arrangements made for them to travel. This would have taken more time to get them out of their country and if Saddam Hussein wanted to inflict punishment or death on many of these Kurdish refugees, they they would have been in close proximity. Saddam Hussein felt that the Kurds were traitors because many had worked for the United States Government in their Country. Many of the Refugees have resettled in Nashville, other cities in Tennessee or in different areas of Michigan. I was with two other Officers from other areas, and we were to take six detainees to Las Vegas for incarceration up there. They had mental problems and were to be evaluated. The detainees we had to take to Las Vegas had a myriad of problems. Al-Tamimi, Ali Jwad, was a disciplinary problem. Al-Shuwail, Mohammed was an assault with a knife. Al-Sobi, Adil Mohammed was a Class A Psychotic.

- One Male 26 years was a Disciplinary case
- One male Assault with a Knife
- Two Others were Class A Psychotics
- One male did not want to assimilate into our culture

• One 60ish Female decided that she had made a mistake and wanted to go back to Iraq

The female above in her six-ties, really surprised me that she would want to return to Iraq. She was Sheikh, Maliha Ibrahim from Iraq. I could not under-stand someone traveling all the way from Iraq to the United States, having an opportunity to leave a controlling country, at that time, it was Saddam Hussein. Listening to Women speak from Muslim Countries is that they do not give their women hardly anything. The Women are not allowed to speak freely, cannot drive, and must always wear the Burqua while in public. There God is not a God of Love like our God is. It is very sad to see the way that they must obey.

The United States People need to realize that when we have people coming into the United States that they need to respect our religion, customs, and ways. They are coming to our Country, not the other way around.

I was surprised that two years ago here in Hawaii, we have had so many Muslims immigrated into our state. They have built a Mosque in Hawaii, and just last year was able to persuade a congressman to vote for a "Muslim Day" in Hawaii. This happens in September. I think that this was a poor choice of month. Many loved ones were lost on 9-11. Sadly the Muslims do not realize that their "Allah" is a false God. Jesus loves us unconditionally, loves those who will come to him. Muslim's do not have this assurance that we have by loving Jesus Christ. They do not know if their Sins are forgiven and they will go to Heaven.

Here in Hawaii, it was unclear whether the allegations against one of their own brothers were confirmed or just hearsay. The 35 years old Moroccan man was accused of threatening the president of the Muslim Association of Hawaii. The Moroccan man, Falah Abdelhak said that he was being "set up" and that members of the mosque were against him. He added that allegations by the Mosque leader Hakim Ouansafi are also false. Abdelhak appeared in the Immigration Court on charges from violating his visa, to living in the United States illegally for fourteen  years. Abdelhak did admit that he had violated his time spent in the United States, but strongly denied that he had threatened anyone. Falah Abdelhak asked the US Immigration Judge if he could have "Voluntary Removal". He was denied because this would mean that he would be free on a bond or bail until he left the United States. Since he had already been in the United States for fourteen years of being illegal, the Judge did not feel that he could be trusted to return. He was put back into the Federal Prison next to the Honolulu Airport until he could be escorted back to his native country.

A Middle Eastern man was charged in the Brooklyn explosives case and was released from the US detention

facility in the state of Washington. He was filing an asylum claim, giving him the right to stay in this country because he was stating that he was fearful for his life. He was stating that Israel was against him. Israel did recognize that this man could be dangerous. His name was Ibrahim Abu Mezer, he was in his twenties, and even New York Mayor, Rudolph Giuliani realized that this man was part of a terror organization. Even Mayor Rudolph Giuliani had to question why when the New York Police had raided their property, Ibrahim Abu Mezer, and Lafi Khalil, both in their early twenties. They were both from Israel's West Bank; both were arrested and wounded during a raid at their Brooklyn apartment early in the morning. Two potential suicide-style explosives were found, according to authorities who have charged them with conspiracy. A note written by Abu Mezer in Arabic, spouted hatred for the Jewish people and Americans as well. Court documents show that Abu Mezer applied for Political Asylum in the United States. He acknowledged being arrested and accused of being a member of a terrorist group, "Hamas". In 1997, the people of Israel had many suicide bombers in their country. This is Holy Ground, as our Lord and Savior; Jesus Christ has walked in these areas. Mezer's case illustrates the frustration that understaffed Border Patrol Officers feel. Abu Mezer agreed to leave voluntarily for Canada. Canada refused to take him back into Canada, and they are not required to accept him because he is not a Canadian Citizen. He had a hearing for an Asylum claim, but he withdrew the request for asylum. No one has heard from him, he agreed to leave the country voluntarily, but the United States has no record of him leaving.

I do think that a harder approach needs to be looked at for our immigration.

My question would be, "If this Country is so bad, and Terrible, why are so many people still coming to the United States. This does not make any sense. The United States has many freedoms that other countries do not have. This is especially true of Middle Eastern countries.

As a Christian nation, I cannot understand why people from other Countries

would want to come here and change our country. It is Ironic that the many people that come here, want to impose their values and religious views on us the Christians. I do not understand how they can be this way. We can hate the sin, but love the sinner. We need to hang on to our heritage as tightly as possible.

I never realized that living in America that we would ever have so many Muslims in the United States of America. I was surprised to do research on this in America. In California alone there is 220 Muslim Mosques. I also found that every state in our country has a least one mosque, and many have more than one. Our Pastor at our Church in Hawaii Explains that the Koran says in their chapters, known as "Suri"s, to Kill the Infidels. We Christians are those Infidels. Many Muslims have converted to Christianity, only to be rejected from their family. Being a Muslim is engrained in their culture.

I pray that they would find the Love of Jesus and it would change their way of doing things and for them to realize that he is a God of Love. When they realize that are God is a God of Love, wants that for all people it should make a difference in their thinking of being a Muslim.